THE NUBIANS

THE NUBIANS

PEOPLE OF
THE ANCIENT NILE

ROBERT STEVEN BIANCHI

Beyond Museum Walls
The Millbrook Press
Brookfield, Connecticut

*For Kyria, Pami Anne, Danny, Joe, Jacqui,
Ursula, Bobby, Brent, Vincent, Vanessa,
Laura, Steven, Alexander, and all the other
children of the world.*

Cover photo: Stone statuettes from the tomb of the Nubian king
Taharka, who ruled in the 600s B.C. They represented servants
who, the Nubians believed, would help the king in the afterlife.
(Courtesy of Museum of Fine Arts, Boston: Museum Expedition)

Photographs courtesy of ALEA: pp. 9, 10, 12, 25, 32, 45, 49,
51, 56; Museum of Fine Arts, Boston: pp. 15, 27 (MFA–Harvard
University Expedition), 39, 41 (Museum Expedition); The Oriental
Institute of The University of Chicago: pp. 17, 23 (both), 35;
The Metropolitan Museum of Art: pp. 20 (Rogers Fund, 1916, access.
no. 16.2.33,.28,.43,.24,.23,.25), 31 (Egyptian Expedition, Rogers
Fund, 1930, access. no. 30.4.21), 53; The British Museum: pp. 37,
39 (top); The Walters Art Gallery, Baltimore: pp. 44, 47 (top);
The Brooklyn Museum: p. 47 (bottom, photo courtesy of ALEA).

Library of Congress Cataloging-in-Publication Data
Bianchi, Robert Steven, 1943–
The Nubians : people of the ancient Nile /
by Robert Steven Bianchi.
p.   cm.
Includes bibliographical references and index.
Summary: Traces the history of the ancient Nubians and
their highly developed civilization along the Nile Valley.
ISBN 1-56294-356-1 (lib. bdg.)
1. Nubia—Civilization—Juvenile literature.   2. Nubians—
Juvenile literature.   [1. Nubia—Civilization.]   I. Title.
DT159.6.N83B53 1994 939'.78—dc20 93-13273 CIP AC

Published by The Millbrook Press
2 Old New Milford Road, Brookfield, Connecticut 06804

Series Editor: Margaret Cooper

CONTENTS

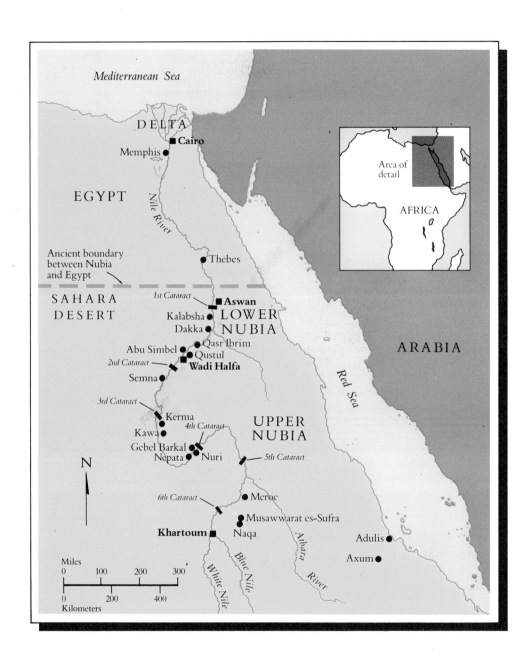

Mediterranean Sea

DELTA

EGYPT

Cairo

Memphis

Nile River

Ancient boundary between Nubia and Egypt

SAHARA DESERT

Thebes

1st Cataract — Aswan

Kalabsha

Dakka

LOWER NUBIA

Abu Simbel — Qasr Ibrim

Qustul

2nd Cataract — Wadi Halfa

Semna

3rd Cataract

Kerma

4th Cataract

Kawa

Gebel Barkal

Nepata — Nuri

5th Cataract

UPPER NUBIA

6th Cataract

Meroe

Musawwarat es-Sufra

Khartoum — Naqa

White Nile

Blue Nile

Athara River

Red Sea

ARABIA

Adulis

Axum

Area of detail

AFRICA

N

Miles
0   100   200   300

0   200   400
Kilometers

INTRODUCTION

THE NUBIANS AND THEIR LAND

About ten thousand years ago, two very important civilizations began to develop in the northeastern corner of Africa. One, the civilization of ancient Egypt, with its pharaohs and pyramids, is perhaps the more famous. This book deals with the other, which also deserves fame: the civilization of Egypt's southern neighbors, the Nubians.

The history and traditions of these Black African people are only now becoming well understood. Much of what scholars know about the early history of the Nubians comes from the records of their ancient Egyptian neighbors, which often mentioned Nubian events. The Nubians had their own spoken languages, but they did not develop their first written language, called Meroitic, until 250 B.C., and no one has yet been able to decipher that ancient language.

Today modern Nubians, the direct descendants of their early forebears, read and write a different language, called Nubian. They are proud of their very long and important history. Many Nubians still live in traditional villages in Egypt and the Republic of Sudan. Although their traditions can be traced back to the dawn of civilization, we are not sure about the origin of the name "Nubia."

The earliest people we can identify as Nubians settled more than ten thousand years ago along the banks of the Nile River between the modern cities of Aswan in Egypt and Khartoum, the capital of

Sudan. Their lands extended north to south for more than 500 miles (800 kilometers) as the crow flies, and almost three times that distance when following the twisting course of the Nile River. These lands range from a dry river valley with little rainfall to savanna, or grassland, with more rainfall.

For convenience, scholars call the northern part of these lands, where the river valley lies, Lower Nubia, and the southern part Upper Nubia. The dividing line is near the modern Egyptian town of Wadi Halfa, which marks today's border between Egypt and Sudan. The "Upper" and "Lower" in the two names refer to the flow of the Nile River. Unlike rivers in the United States, the Nile flows from south to north. Thus Upper Nubia lies upstream of Lower Nubia in the north. Keeping in mind the direction of the river's flow will help you remember the positions of Upper and Lower Nubia. These divisions are important for historical reasons, because Lower Nubia and Egypt shared a common border and often warred over it.

THE NUBIANS AND THE NILE ▪ Throughout their long history, the Nubians have been dependent on the Nile River, which cuts its narrow channel through the honey-colored sandstone cliffs of their homeland. A narrow strip of fertile land on each side of the Nile, bounded by the sandstone cliffs and watered by the river, was home to the Nubians.

At six places the Nile is interrupted by cataracts, where huge boulders of granite, a very hard stone, have been pushed by natural forces to the earth's surface through the softer Nubian sandstone. A cataract is a waterfall or a steep stretch of rapids. The rapids that develop as the Nile flows over the boulders prevent ships from sailing over the cataracts.

The Nile would flood each year during the month of August. At that time, heavy rains in central Africa and snow melting on moun-

Many present-day Nubians, like this young girl, live in traditional villages in Egypt and the Republic of Sudan.

**Archaeologists uncover an ancient
site. The work often goes slowly
because it must be done with care.**

taintops in Ethiopia would fill the river and cause it to overflow its banks in Nubia. Each year the receding floodwaters would leave behind a layer of silt, or very fertile mud, in which the Nubians could plant their main crops of wheat and barley. During the growing season, they could irrigate the crops with the river's waters. This was especially important in Lower Nubia, where less rain falls than in Upper Nubia. But the Nubians had to build their villages at some distance from the river, so that their homes would not be washed away in the annual floods.

The Nile was an important resource for the Nubians from the earliest periods of their history. It provided them with water for drinking, cooking, and washing. They also could use its waters to refresh their herds of cattle and flocks of sheep and goats. And the Nile itself was always a source of food, because the Nubians were skilled in catching the fish in its waters and in hunting birds, especially ducks, that nested in its marshes.

As a result, it was along the river that the Nubians developed their civilization. Various phases, or periods, of that civilization have been recovered by archaeologists. Archaeologists are specially trained men and women who excavate, or dig up, ancient cities and other places built or occupied by people in the past, and then study the objects buried by the sands of time. Many of the objects from Nubia found by archaeologists are now on view in museums throughout North America. Perhaps you will be able to visit the Nubian galleries in one of the museums listed at the end of this book.

The hard work of archaeologists and the people who work in those museums has helped us to write the story of the Nubians that follows. There are still many gaps in our knowledge. The links between periods of Nubian history are not always clear, for example. The chapters in this book attempt to present Nubian culture as accurately as the known facts permit.

The early Nubians carved pictures of animals into sandstone, leaving a record thousands of years old.

CHAPTER ONE

THE EARLIEST NUBIANS

The very first people of whom we have any archaeological evidence in this area of northeastern Africa have been identified as Nubians. About ten thousand years ago, these early Nubians, resting on the sandstone hills overlooking the Nile River, began to draw and to carve images on the smooth rock surfaces of the mountainsides.

At first these images were simple designs made up of curving and parallel lines, sometimes with dots. As time passed, the designs became more complicated. The artists began to carve images of wild animals, including giraffes, elephants, and gazelles. Occasionally there are figures of humans capturing some of these wild animals with lassos, like the ropes that cowboys use.

These scenes, created by Nubians, represent very early examples of African rock art. They are similar to even older scenes found in Europe, in the caves of southern France and Spain. Some scholars think that their purpose was magical. By making images of animals they were hunting, perhaps the Nubians hoped to gain the cooperation of the animals' spirits and assure abundant game.

In addition to hunting near the Nile, where they also caught fish and water birds, some of these early Nubians probably roamed the land, hunting for other beasts and gathering edible plants. Moving from place to place as hunter-gatherers, they lived in temporary tentlike shelters made from either the hides of animals that they hunted or grasses and reeds that they collected.

With the passing of time, the people in Upper Nubia in the south, particularly in the neighborhood of Khartoum, domesticated long-horned cattle. That is, they tamed cattle and began to raise these animals in herds. The Nubians began to picture these animals in their rock art. Similar engravings of such cattle have been found in the mountains rising beside the Sahara Desert. These pictures suggest to archaeologists that the early Nubian herders set out on seasonal drives in search of lands where their cattle could graze. On these drives the Nubians developed contacts with the people of northern and central Africa.

As herds of cattle became a main source of Nubian wealth and importance, about eight thousand years ago, the Nubians gradually stopped living in temporary shelters and began to build permanent settlements. Traces of these very early villages have been found near Khartoum. The Nubians had not yet begun to grow crops or to use writing. But unlike many of their neighbors in the early civilizations of Asia and the ancient Near East, they were skilled potters. The Nubian potters would shape vessels and jars from clay and fire them in kilns, or ovens. These vessels and jars were used as pots for cooking, as dishes and cups for eating and drinking, and as containers for storing a variety of foodstuffs and other things.

FARMERS AND MERCHANTS ▪ About six thousand years ago, the Nubians learned how to farm. They grew wheat and barley, which they used for baking bread and brewing beer. They cultivated date-palm trees. As farmers, they now began to give up the ways of the hunter-gatherers and herders, who moved from place to place. More and more they lived in permanent villages.

**The early Nubians were skilled
potters, as these examples show.**

As their farms prospered and their villages grew, some Nubians became richer and more powerful than their neighbors. These wealthier Nubians soon became leaders of their villages. In time, one or another of these leaders gained control of several villages, which were then united under one ruler and formed a state. This took place in Lower Nubia by about 3100 B.C.

By uniting, these Nubians were able to make better use of resources, such as clay for making pottery and the fuel needed for the kilns in which pots were baked. This helped industries to develop. Some villages grew into towns, serving as capitals for the rulers. Merchants traveled to neighboring states to barter, or exchange, products (money had not yet been invented). Soldiers protected the trade routes. The age of specialization arrived: Nubian children could now grow up to be farmers, herders, potters, merchants, soldiers, or rulers.

Qustul was an important town during this period. It was probably ruled by a king who was shown in art as a powerful baboonlike animal standing on a boat. The Nubians, like the people of other civilizations, may have considered the baboon to be wise and so made it a symbol of one of their gods or goddesses. The Nubian king was associated with this baboon deity. Such scenes in art suggest that by this time the Nubians had developed a complex religion. Many Nubians no doubt served as high priests and priestesses at temples in Nubian towns.

The king and his court probably controlled the distribution of food and the markets where pottery and other products were bartered. They commanded armies that defended the king against challengers. And they controlled trade with the Nubians' neighbors to the north and south. Today, we call the Nubians of this period the *A-Group culture*, to set them apart from those who came later.

Archaeologists have learned much about the Nubians of this time by studying objects from their graves. When a Nubian died, a relative carefully laid the body in a grave, placed on its side in a sleeping position with the knees pulled up to the chest. Because the Nubians believed in an afterlife, graves were equipped with what might be needed in the next life, and the body would often be clothed.

Loincloths, or short skirtlike garments wrapped around the waist and reaching to the knees, were worn. These were woven from linen or made of leather tanned from the hides of cattle and other animals. Nubians also wore leather belts, sandals, and caps. Burials show that the Nubians of this time favored jewelry, too. Bracelets made from bone, ivory, and colored stones and necklaces made by stringing together tiny beads were popular. The graves also con-

A Nubian artist of the A-Group culture
created this wonderful terra-cotta
(baked clay) head of a hippopotamus.

tained the stone tools and weapons that the dead person might have used in life, as well as an assortment of pottery vessels for food and drink. After the body and these objects were buried, the more elaborate graves would be covered with a circular structure made of stones. Some would even be marked with a stela, or memorial stone, but without writing on it.

The Nubians of the A-Group culture became skilled merchants, trading far and wide with their neighbors, because Nubia lay on the trade routes along which the products of Africa passed. Elephant ivory and the skins of exotic African animals such as the leopard were obtained in trade from the Nubians' neighbors to the south. These goods, as well as examples of Nubian pottery, have been found in excavations in Egypt to the north. The Nubians apparently traded these items with the Egyptians for cheese, oil, honey, and linen cloth, products that they needed but lacked.

This trade helped both the Nubians and the Egyptians. But by 2800 B.C., trading agreements were replaced by military rivalry. Nubian and Egyptian armies clashed over control of the trade routes and the right to rule Lower Nubia. In the end, the forces of Egypt were victorious. The fighting brought great destruction, and many lives were lost. The Nubians retreated to the south, far beyond the reach of the Egyptian army.

THE B-GROUP ▪ Archaeologists have difficulty tracing the events in Nubia following the collapse of the A-Group culture. It appears that a strong and independent group of Nubians may have lived near the Third Cataract of the Nile between 2800 and 2000 B.C. These Nubians are sometimes called the *B-Group culture*. But a great deal of archaeological excavation and study must be done before we can know more about this culture.

CHAPTER TWO

MERCENARIES, CATTLE HERDERS, AND WEALTH AND GLORY

During the course of their long, rich history, the Nubians developed several different cultures. In fact, archaeologists have found evidence for three Nubian cultures during the period from 2000 to 1500 B.C. All three were Nubian, but each had its own characteristics. They are known as the Pan-Grave people, the C-Group culture, and the Kerma Culture.

THE PAN-GRAVE PEOPLE: MERCENARIES ▪ About 2200 B.C. a group of Nubians, probably nomadic tribes who roamed the deserts east of the Nile River, settled in Lower Nubia. Famed as archers, these Nubians would seek work as mercenaries, or paid soldiers, in the Egyptian army. Many adopted the customs and dress of their Egyptian officers, whom they faithfully served. Because they were nomadic and hired out their services, we have few remains of their culture. However, these Nubians did bury their dead in distinctively shaped, shallow graves with flat bottoms and rounded sides. Because this shape reminded archaeologists of the shape of a frying pan, they called the culture of these people the *Pan-Grave culture*.

These Nubians valued certain animal skulls to which the horns were still attached. One collection of about two dozen of these skulls includes the horns and frontal bones of long-horned cattle, gazelles,

These animal skulls, with horns attached, came from a Pan-Grave cemetery. The Pan-Grave Nubians painted the skulls and valued them highly, but archaeologists are not sure how they were used.

goats, and different kinds of sheep. Each of the skulls had been painted with designs in red and black colors, which the Pan-Grave Nubians created by dipping their fingers into either soot, collected from a fire, or red ocher, a kind of clay rich in iron ore. What were these skulls used for? One idea is that the Pan-Grave Nubians hung decorated skulls over the entrances of their huts or tents to protect their homes magically from harm.

THE C-GROUP PEOPLE: CATTLE HERDERS ▪ Because they were no-mads seeking work as bowmen, the Pan-Grave Nubians did not lay claim to the lands where they traveled. But by the year 2000 B.C. a second group of Nubians, belonging to what archaeologists call the *C-Group culture*, moved into their ancestral lands in Lower Nubia, south of the modern Egyptian city of Aswan. These settlers soon occupied the territory once the home of the A-Group culture. The newly arrived people were mainly farmers and herders who excelled in raising cattle and lived in villages. We do not know much about their government, but archaeological finds suggest that they lived a more settled village life than the A-Group people. Like A-Group settlements, their villages were not surrounded by walls. Their homes, built partly of stone, usually had just one room, but larger structures with several round rooms have also been excavated. Both types of houses were built on foundations of stone slabs. The floors were covered with a mixture of pebbles and packed mud. Wooden beams supported the roof.

These Nubians buried their dead in graves that they usually covered with a tumulus, or large round structure, made of stone. Such tombs are typical of Nubian burials and are not related in any way to the famous pyramids of Egypt. A Nubian tumulus might be quite high, and might be marked by a stela decorated with carvings of long-horned cattle. So important were cattle as a symbol of wealth and power that several were often sacrificed in honor of the deceased person. Groups of skulls of these sacrificed animals have been found among the grave furnishings of the wealthier people. The C-Group Nubians also carved images of these animals in their rock art and created statuettes of them in terra-cotta, a kind of baked clay.

The Nubians of the C-Group culture also created delightful terra-cotta statuettes of women. These figurines, just 4 inches (10 centimeters) tall, generally show the woman in a seated position.

They have networks of lines on their surface that may show body decoration, in the form of either tattoos or scarification, an intentional cutting of the skin to produce a pattern of scars. Today, many Nubian women still practice scarification, particularly on the face. In addition, the C-Group people created pottery that is truly extraordinary for its forms and decoration.

The Nubians of the C-Group culture lived side by side with the Egyptians, who had built large forts at places such as Semna, between the Second and Third cataracts. The C-Group Nubians and the Egyptians manning these forts traded goods with one another and seemed to live in a spirit of peaceful and mutual cooperation. Both recognized the fact that some Pan-Grave Nubians were fighting on the side of the Egyptian army for pay against other Nubians, particularly against those of the Kerma Culture.

THE KERMA CULTURE: WEALTH AND GLORY ▪ The Egyptians had built their forts as bases from which they could trade with a third group of Nubians that was living in Upper Nubia at this time. This group had established a remarkable empire in the south, beyond the reach of the Egyptian forts, in their own homelands between the Third and Fourth cataracts of the Nile River. They belonged to what archaeologists call the *Kerma Culture*, named after Kerma, their capital city.

The rulers of Kerma had gradually established regular trade routes to the interior of Africa. All of Africa's luxury goods were imported into Kerma and from there passed, through a series of middlemen, to the islands of the eastern Mediterranean Sea and beyond. The goods included exotic animals such as the leopard and giraffe, as well as their skins; ivory in the form of elephant tusks; ostrich eggs and feathers; hardwoods such as ebony; and gold in vast quantities. Through the wealth built up by this exchange of goods, the Nubians of Kerma became exceedingly rich.

A Nubian artist carved an entire herd of cattle onto the surface of this remarkable pottery bowl, which dates from the C-Group culture.

This bronze or copper hand mirror, found at Qustul, was made between the 16th and 13th centuries B.C.

Like the earlier A-Group people, the Kerma Nubians wore leather garments, made from the tanned hides of their herds and flocks and from the skins of gazelles. Some of their clothing was dyed red. The loincloths of the men and skirts of the women were decorated with beadwork in diamond-shaped patterns. Some clothing was made of leather of different colors stitched together like a patchwork quilt. Belts and sandals with laces were also worn. Both men and women covered their heads with caps decorated by sewing on designs made from pieces of mica, a shiny, mirrorlike mineral. These designs might vary from patterns of rectangles to the shapes of various animals such as giraffes, birds, or mythological creatures like a hippopotamus with the tail of a crocodile.

Kerma, the capital, was a glorious city, reflecting the wealth and prestige of its people. The king lived in a large, round palace, built of reeds and timbers, that looked something like the houses of more recent African kings. Some people lived in smaller versions of this grand, round home, while others lived in square homes. Many of these homes, both large and small, had porches or verandas that gave shelter from the hot African sun. Mud-brick platforms, built into the walls, may have served as tables, chairs, and benches. Occasionally other pieces of furniture might be woven from reeds and wicker, the way they are still fashioned in parts of Africa today. Instead of closets, the Nubians stored their garments and other possessions in boxes and chests. These were often covered with colorfully woven mats and trays. Some of the wealthier Nubians of the Kerma Culture had wooden beds, designed just like the beds used by the modern Nubians today.

Of all the buildings that have survived from the city of Kerma, none is more striking than the huge mud-brick structure known to modern Nubians as the Deffufa. The Deffufa may have been a manu-

Although worn down by the passing centuries, the Deffufa is still impressive. The mud-brick structure at Kerma rises five stories tall and was used for many purposes.

eastern Egypt. Together the Hyksos and the Nubians of Kerma planned to take control of the entire country of Egypt.

These plans were not realized. The Egyptians living in the city of Thebes rallied their countrymen and women and began a series of decisive military campaigns. These wars ended about 1550 B.C. By that time, the Egyptians, having defeated the Hyksos, also stormed into Nubia. They recaptured the Egyptian forts and marched against the city of Kerma. Soon the Egyptians attacked that city and destroyed its defensive walls.

The fall of this important city marked the end of the Kerma Culture. The Egyptians were then able to control the area as far south as the Fourth Cataract. The Pan-Grave Nubians, many of whom took part in these wars, doubtless went back to their traditional nomadic ways. Some may even have died serving in the army of Nubians from Kerma. Some of their descendants continued to work as policemen for the Egyptians of the New Kingdom, as this period of ancient Egyptian history is called.

CHAPTER THREE

NUBIA AND EGYPT

The Egyptian defeat of the Nubians at Kerma and the presence of the Egyptian army as far south as the Fourth Cataract forced the Nubians to come into more and more contact with the Egyptians. As a result, many Nubians, on the surface at least, appeared to abandon their own customs and traditions in favor of those of their Egyptian overlords. Many Nubians, for example, were given Egyptian names and wore Egyptian-style clothes. The temples built in Nubia during this time are purely Egyptian in their design and decoration.

To retain their control over Nubia, the Egyptians created a special position, called "the king's son of Kush." (Kush was one of the ancient Egyptian names for Nubia.) This official, who was not necessarily an actual son of the Egyptian king, ruled Nubia as a kind of governor. He was responsible for the administration of Nubia and was always on the lookout for possible signs of revolt.

One of the most famous king's sons of Kush was an official named Huy, who lived during the time of the boy-king Tutankhamen, about 1320 B.C. Because the Egyptians believed that life after death would be a continuation of life on Earth, many Egyptians decorated the walls of their tombs with scenes of events in their lives. Among the paintings decorating the tomb of Huy is an interesting one that illustrates his role as king's son of Kush.

This scene shows that the king's son of Kush made sure that the Nubians brought the treasures of Africa into Egypt on a regular basis. In two registers, or rows, beginning at the bottom left, we see a group of Nubians leading a herd of their famous long-horned cattle. Atop the head of each animal is a sculpture of a Nubian head, perhaps portraying the wealthy Nubian whose herds that animal belongs to. A hand-shaped cover over the sharp end of each horn protects the people nearby. The cattle follow a giraffe, and Nubians bearing trays filled with gold in the form of doughnut-shaped rings or bags of gold dust.

On the top register, at the left, one of the Nubian women carries her child in a Nubian version of a backpack; children today are often carried the same way. Ahead walk five Nubian warriors. Their hair is decorated with feathers, and they wear the decorated leather loincloths typical of Nubian male fashion. They carry *sheyba*, staves of wood that symbolize authority the way a scepter does. But their *sheyba* have been tied to their wrists and necks to show their submission to the king of Egypt.

Next comes a Nubian princess, cooled by an ostrich-feather fan, riding in a chariot pulled by oxen. With her are two Nubians bearing panther skins and more gold. Four more Nubians, their hands down in gestures of respect, stand behind the princess, who is shown a second time. Her jewelry includes a crown, an enormous earring, and a necklace called a broad collar. Two more high-ranking Nubians, shown with their bows and arrow-filled quivers over their heads, kneel and raise their arms in adoration.

Many sons of important Nubians were brought to Egypt, where they lived at the court of the Egyptian pharaoh and were taught the language and customs of the Egyptians. There they would also make friends with Egyptian children their own age. As they

A wall painting from the tomb of Huy, an
Egyptian official who governed Nubia, shows
Nubians delivering tribute to Egypt.

Statues at Karnak, near Thebes in Egypt, depict
the god Amun as a ram. They show that Nubian
beliefs influenced the religion of ancient Egypt.

grew up, these bonds of friendship would increase. When they were grown, these young Nubians returned to their homes, carrying with them fond memories of Egypt. In this way, the pharaohs of Egypt sought to cement the ties between the two peoples. Because of this policy of acculturation, or the forcing of Egyptian manners and customs on others, it is almost impossible to discover what the lifestyles of the Nubians were like during this period.

Nevertheless, in the case of religion, we can learn about Nubian beliefs and see how these beliefs influenced the Egyptians. For long periods the ancient Egyptians had worshiped a god named Amun and had made images of this deity as a man wearing a crown topped by two tall ostrich feathers. Amun was also sacred to the Nubians. As early as the Kerma Culture, Nubian Amun was worshiped in the form of a ram. The god appears in this form in images at the most sacred site of Gebel Barkal, or holy mountain, near the city of Napata in Upper Nubia, between the Third and Fourth cataracts. Through contact with the Nubians, particularly at this site, the Egyptians gradually began to depict their god as the Nubian ram.

THE NUBIAN PHARAOHS OF EGYPT ▪ Despite Egyptian attempts to change them, many Nubians steadfastly continued to follow their own traditions. At the holy mountain, Gebel Barkal, the sacred site deep within their own territory in Upper Nubia, they honored their gods and paid special respect to Amun in the form of a ram. In Napata, their capital city, the Nubians continued to speak their own language and observe their ancient customs. They also kept their armies at the ready.

About 800 B.C., these Nubians heard reports that the central government of Egypt was crumbling. Petty Egyptian princes were fighting among themselves, each seeking to become pharaoh of the land. Some Nubians may have visited Egypt and seen with their own eyes how civil strife was causing neglect of the temples and allowing them to fall into ruin. The situation was serious. No Egyptian appeared strong enough to take control of the country.

King Piye ▪ And so it was that on a fateful day in 724 B.C., a Nubian king named Piye, sometimes called Piankhy, "the living one," decided to do what no Egyptian was capable of doing at that time. He gathered his troops and his advisers and decided then and there to invade Egypt, so that he might restore order to that land.

Marching north at the head of his Nubian army, King Piye traveled through Lower Nubia and reached the frontier town of Aswan. From there he led his army to Thebes, once the capital of Egypt. As a dutiful and pious king, Piye paid homage to the god Amun. He then focused his attention on the petty princes of the Egyptian delta (the large triangular area where the Nile broadens into marshes and channels, between modern Cairo and the Mediterranean Sea).

These princes temporarily set aside their rivalries to unite their forces against Piye. They chose as their leader a general named Tefnakht. Piye marched against Tefnakht and defeated him. The king's account of the campaign describes him as "raging like a panther" and states that his troops "rained upon the battlefield like a cloudburst." Though fierce in battle, the Nubian Piye was not ruthless. He avoided killing his enemies whenever possible, granting them life in exchange for their pledge of support.

During the campaign, Tefnakht had mistreated his war horses. When Piye learned of this abuse, he sternly scolded Tefnakht and demanded the horses as presents, because he was so fond of those animals. Because of the Nubian belief in an afterlife in which things buried with the dead would accompany that person forever, King

This bronze statue
of a Nubian king was
made about 700 B.C.

Piye was buried together with eight of his best horses when he died in 716 B.C. Each was decorated with ostrich feathers on its head and a blanket of beaded nets over its back. The horse trappings included amulets, or charms against evil, made of faience and of silver.

King Shabako and the Assyrians ▪ Piye and his descendants would rule most of Egypt until about 660 B.C. We know these rulers as the Twenty-fifth Dynasty of Egypt. However, neither Piye nor his brother and successor, Shabako (or Shabaka), could gain control of the Egyptian delta. Shabako established a religious and administrative capital at Thebes in Egypt. But he officially ruled the recently conquered territory of Egypt from Napata, far to the south. There he and his court continued to speak their native, ancient language (not the Nubian that is spoken today). Because that ancient language was never written, however, Shabako ordered the use of Egyptian hieroglyphs, or picture writing, for royal decrees and prayers.

Shabako was proud of his Nubian traditions and customs and commissioned several bronze statuettes portraying him with typical Nubian accessories.

To promote worship of Amun, King Shabako continued the practice of appointing a Nubian princess as a special priestess of that god. Her official title was "the god's wife of Amun." Shepenwepet was the name of one of these Nubian princess-priestesses. A second was Amenirdis the Elder, a sister of Piye.

At the same time that he was involved with the cult of the god Amun at Thebes, the Nubian king Shabako also had to deal with the Assyrians, one of the ancient world's most warlike peoples. They lived in the region that is now Iraq. The Assyrians were trying to conquer the lands to their east and south, threatening Egypt and Israel.

King Taharka, the Warrior Hero ▪ Shabako died and was succeeded by his son, Shebitko (or Shebitku). His rule, from 698 to 690 B.C., was spent preparing for war with the Assyrians. Upon his death, his younger brother, Taharka, became king. Taharka is one of the most famous of all the Nubian kings, and one of the most beloved. When it became clear that he would be crowned king of Egypt in 690 B.C., he decided to send for his mother, who was living in the palace at Napata. She made the journey of more than 1,200 miles (1,930 kilometers) to the Egyptian city of Memphis (near modern Cairo) to be at his side on this festive occasion. Taharka recorded his mother's feelings in a hieroglyphic inscription: "She was thrilled to see me upon the throne of Egypt!"

King Taharka is shown as a human-headed lion, or sphinx, in this statue from a temple at Kawa, south of Kerma. The sphinx represents the king's power and strength—qualities that he often displayed on the battlefield.

Realizing that the Assyrians would soon be attacking Egypt, Taharka wanted his troops to train and prepare for battle. As part of that training, he organized a kind of marathon requiring his troops to run a race of 30 miles (48 kilometers) across the desert. Because the days were very hot, he ordered his men to run at night when the air was cooler. The race took at least five hours to complete, and Taharka, mounted on his horse, observed his men. He was so pleased with all their performances that he awarded prizes to the winner and losers alike.

In 671 B.C., the Assyrians decided to invade Egypt, having previously overrun Israel. Taharka fought valiantly in the front lines, but the Assyrians conquered the city of Memphis. Taharka was forced to flee to Thebes. Eventually, despite Taharka's courageous defense of Egypt, the Assyrians overran the country and may even have reached Thebes. Taharka and his forces were forced to retreat to Napata, deep in Upper Nubian territory.

Despite these defeats, Taharka's valor on the battlefield was well known. He was praised not only by Nubians and Egyptians but also by the Israelites, who recognized his ability to stand up against the might of Assyria. The Nubian king Taharka is even mentioned twice in the Old Testament as a defender of Israel against the Assyrians.

Taharka died in Nubia in 664 B.C. He was buried at Nuri. Because he had ruled over Egypt, it was decided that he would be buried in a pyramid, as were Egyptian pharaohs, and not in a tumulus, as were earlier rulers of Nubia. Other members of his dynasty were also buried in pyramids. As a result, there are more royal pyramids in Nubia than in all of Egypt.

In the tradition of the burials of the rulers of Kerma, Taharka's funerary equipment included a bed. But by this time the Kerma Culture's practice of sacrificing human beings had ended. Instead more than one thousand servant statuettes, called *ushabtis*, sculpted in many different types of stone, were placed in the tomb.

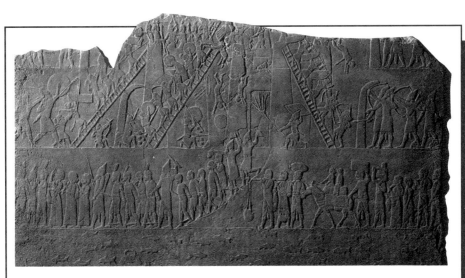

A relief from the palace of the Assyrian king Ashurbanipal at Nineveh shows the Assyrians storming the walls of an Egyptian city. Nubian prisoners, their hands bound behind their backs, are marched away.

Stone figurines of servants, such as this one, were buried with King Taharka. The Nubians believed that they would magically come to life in the next world, to perform specific tasks for him.

THE KINGDOM OF NAPATA AND THE RETURN TO NUBIA • Taharka was succeeded by his nephew, Tanwetamani (or Tantamani), who tried to invade Egypt and win it back from the Assyrians. But when the Nubians marched once again into Egypt, the forces of the Assyrian king Ashurbanipal proved too strong. Tanwetamani was driven from Egypt shortly after 664 B.C. and returned to Nubia. He ruled there as king until his death in 653 B.C. Because Egypt had now been lost, his successors turned their backs on the problems of Egypt and devoted their time and energies to enriching and improving Upper Nubia, their cherished homeland. Their capital city was Napata.

The Nubian kings of Napata ruled for four centuries, until about 270 B.C. During that time they established fixed rules for the transfer of power. All future Nubian kings and queens had to be the sons and daughters of a reigning queen, who was usually the sister of the current king.

The Nubian kings of Napata also gained control over the trade routes to the south, which the rulers of Kerma had earlier pioneered. Thus the wealth of Nubia, which had long come from trade, remained great. The wealth and power of the Napatan kings are reflected in a colossal statue, originally covered with gold, showing King Aspelta, who ruled at the start of the fifth century B.C. And Nubian artisans continued to display their skill in creating luxury objects made of precious materials.

The Nubians honored the god Amun as their father and supreme deity. They turned to him for answers to all of life's many problems. For example, they did not know whether Aspelta or one of his brothers should become king of Napata. The priests, acting on behalf of the god, declared that Amun had decided in Aspelta's favor. Every Nubian, king and commoner alike, was obliged to follow the advice of this all-powerful god.

A huge statue of King Aspelta shows him with the royal ostrich plumes on top of his Nubian cap, which is decorated with images of two royal cobras. On his chest are traces of a lanyard from which ram's head pendants once hung.

Because they claimed to be in direct contact with the god Amun, the priests reserved the right to interpret his messages and to decide matters of policy. As a result, the priests of Napata became very powerful. It was not long before they showed their power in another way. When they were dissatisfied with the way a king was ruling, the priests claimed that the god Amun had ordered him to commit suicide.

So strong was the authority of Amun that many kings actually obeyed this order. But when the priests of Amun reported that the god ordered the death of King Arkamani, who ruled about 270 B.C., he took matters into his own hands. Gathering his troops, King Arkamani marched against the priests and is reported to have killed them all. In order to rid himself of their influence, Arkamani moved the capital from Napata to the city of Meroë, farther to the south in Upper Nubia, between the Fifth and Sixth cataracts. That move signaled the end of the kingdom of Napata and the beginning of the glorious kingdom of Meroë.

CHAPTER FOUR

THE KINGDOM OF MEROË

Nubians ruled from the city of Meroë, deep within Upper Nubia, for more than six hundred years. The Meroites, as these Nubians are called, maintained a powerful army. With the help of their faithful soldiers, the Meroitic kings dominated the trade routes to Africa's interior. They even controlled some of the ports along the Red Sea, where ships often docked with cargoes of spices from the East. Once again, the luxury products of Africa, including exotic animals and their pelts, ivory, ebony, and gold, were gathered by the Meroites and traded with their neighbors.

Egypt was Meroë's most important trading partner. Beginning about 300 B.C., Egypt was ruled by the Ptolemies, a dynasty named in honor of a general, Ptolemy, who had served in the army of the Greek conqueror Alexander the Great. The close trading ties between Egypt and the kingdom of Meroë brought benefits to both sides. In fact, shortly after he moved the capital from Napata to Meroë, King Arkamani worked with a king of Egypt to pay for construction of temples in the Lower Nubian villages of Dakka and Kalabsha. The Nubian god Dedun, who represented the four points of the compass, was even worshiped in Egyptian temples.

Despite these good relations with their neighbors, the Meroites never forgot their Nubian origins. They did more, perhaps, than

The lion-headed god Apedemak was the protector of the kingdom of Meroë.

their ancestors to promote and encourage the flowering of Nubian traditions. They still worshiped Amun in the form of a ram, and they also honored other Nubian deities. These included the all-important god Apedemak, often shown as a lion or a lion-headed man. Apedemak was the god of war, who granted the Meroitic armies victory. He often appears holding either elephants or lions on leashes.

At the site of Musawwarat es-Sufra, the Meroites built an elaborate religious complex, now called the Great Enclosure. The many depictions of elephants decorating this sanctuary suggest to archaeologists that the Great Temple here was the center of a Nubian elephant cult that attracted thousands of worshipers. On special holidays, the Nubians would throng to the Great Temple from all parts of the kingdom of Meroë. Courtyards within the Great Enclosure served as a kind of hotel for the worshipers. There were even special places for the camels and donkeys that carried the pilgrims to the celebration. The site also contained several reservoirs, called *hafirs*, some of which measured almost 750 feet (228 meters) in diameter. These held enough water to meet the needs of the priests, the worshipers, and their animals.

The Great Enclosure at Musawwarat es-Sufra may have been a religious sanctuary that drew thousands of worshipers.

The kings and queens of Meroë favored traditional Nubian costumes. A king or queen usually wore a long robe draped with a fringed shawl. The edges of these garments often were decorated with long tassels. Depending on the occasion, rulers could wear one of any number of fancy headdresses. Both kings and queens wore elaborate earrings, necklaces, bracelets, armlets, and anklets. Rings were extremely popular, especially large shield rings that covered several fingers.

NEW IDEAS, NEW TOOLS ▪ The Meroites were among the most inventive of all the Nubians. It has been suggested that their artisans were among the first to smelt, or extract by heat, iron from the ore found in Nubia. Moreover, the Meroites were the first Nubians to develop a written language. It used an alphabet of twenty-three letters that could be written either as pictures, comparable perhaps to our printed texts today, or in a more abstract, cursive form, comparable to the script we write by hand with a pen or pencil. Many Nubian monuments have texts written in this unique Nubian alphabet. We are not sure how this written language relates to the languages spoken by the earlier Nubians. Scholars have been able to identify the names of Meroitic rulers and deities in these inscriptions, but even with the help of computers, the written Nubian language has not been fully deciphered.

During the first century A.D. other technological inventions were brought into the kingdom of Meroë. The *sakieh*, an important device used for irrigating crops, was introduced into the kingdom of Meroë from Egypt. It consists of a wooden wheel, very much like a wagon wheel, with a pottery jar attached to the outer rim wherever a spoke ends. The wheel is connected to a series of gears and turned by yoked animals, usually oxen, that walk around a well in a circle. As the wheel turns, the jars are lowered into the well one after the other.

In this carving, King Tamyidamani wears the long robe, fringed shawl, and elaborate headdress typical of Meroë's rulers. The carving also shows Meroitic writing, which has yet to be deciphered.

The delicate design on this Meroitic vase shows a running antelope.

They fill with water, are raised to the surface, and spill their water into an irrigation channel. Using such waterwheels, Meroitic farmers increased their annual harvests.

The Meroites continued the time-honored traditions of the Nubian potters. Their vases were well made and decorated with a variety of very pleasing, artistic designs—images of animals, such as snakes or giraffes, and even of Meroites as archers or dancers at a party.

THE IMPORTANCE OF WOMEN ▪ One of the most fascinating aspects of Meroitic Nubia is the importance given to women, particularly the queen. This may reflect central African traditions. The queens of Meroë were powerful forces in the courts of their husbands and sons, providing advice. Nubian princesses could also become the sole rulers of the kingdom of Meroë. The name for these ruler-queens was Candake (or Candace). The word survives today in English as the woman's name "Candace." One of the most famous of all the Candakes was the Nubian woman generally identified as Amanirenas, who lived shortly after 30 B.C.

At that time Egypt, ruled by the Ptolemies, had recently been conquered by the Roman emperor Augustus. Augustus realized that the border between Ptolemaic Egypt and the kingdom of Meroë was located at Aswan. He stationed a garrison of his best soldiers in that area to collect taxes from the Meroitic subjects living in Lower Nubia, who were ruled by Queen Amanirenas.

The queen summoned her husband, Teritekas, and their son, Prince Akinidad, to help her decide what to do. The Candake explained that the Nubians had always enjoyed peace and friendship with the Ptolemies of Egypt. She was angered that the Roman emperor Augustus had now violated the peaceful relations by imposing taxes on the Lower Nubians. Although she intended to organize a military strike against the Romans, Amanirenas realized that she had to wait for the right moment.

That moment came soon, when the Roman legions in distant Arabia were attacked. Augustus, realizing that he needed reinforcements to assist in the fighting there, ordered most of the soldiers stationed at Aswan to march off to Arabia. As soon as the Roman soldiers withdrew from Aswan, the angry Lower Nubians revolted. Armed with axes, spears, and swords and carrying ox-hide shields, the Lower Nubians were joined by soldiers from Meroë. Together they damaged much of the Roman fortifications and toppled the statues of the Roman emperor Augustus. The Meroites left the few defeated Roman soldiers with a message from the queen, urging the Romans to abandon their plans to tax Lower Nubia.

The pyramids of Meroë.

Before returning to Meroë, the queen's generals removed the head from a life-sized bronze statue of Augustus, which they had knocked down earlier. They carried this head back home with them. There, in a special ceremony, the Meroites buried the head in an underground chamber beneath the doorway of the queen's palace. Each time she entered and left the palace, the Candake would tread upon the buried image of Augustus. By stepping on his head, the queen was symbolically re-enacting the defeat of the Emperor Augustus and magically keeping his powers in check.

A short time later, Augustus learned about the attack. He then ordered his legions, fresh from their victory over his enemy in Arabia, to return to Aswan and prepare for war against the Meroites. At first the Romans were successful. They forced the Meroitic army to retreat to the city of Napata. Then, angered by the defeat, the Candake Amanirenas personally took charge of her troops.

Marching at the head of her army, Amanirenas reached the strategic city of Qasr Ibrim, south of the Egyptian city of Aswan. There she confronted the Roman general Petronius, who told her that Emperor Augustus was willing to lay aside his arms if Amanirenas would negotiate a settlement with him. The Candake agreed. She sent her ambassadors to the Greek island of Samos to meet with the representatives of Rome. The Roman historian Strabo records the results of that meeting with these words:

The Meroitic Ambassadors obtained everything for which they asked. And the Roman Emperor even remitted the taxes that he had levied on the region.

Although no images of the Candake Amenirenas survive, we can get an idea of her appearance by looking at the pylon, or gateway, of the Temple to the god Apedemak at Naqa.

**A temple gateway at Naqa shows a
Candake, or ruler-queen, on the right.**

On this pylon the wife of King Natakamani is shown as a woman whose full figure represents a Meroitic ideal of female beauty. She wears the traditional elaborate costume of long robes and shawls decorated with tassels. In keeping with the warrior tradition of the Meroitic ruler-queens, she leans forward, her raised hand wielding a sharp sword. With it she is about to behead the prisoners whom she holds by the hair in her tight grasp. Her might is symbolized by the figure of the lion at her feet, which lunges forward and paws the enemies with its sharp claws.

Thanks to the efforts of Queen Amanirenas, the Roman emperor Augustus was obliged to show special favor to the Lower Nubians. Shortly after he had canceled the taxes, Augustus decided to pay for the building of several temples in Lower Nubia. One of these, at the village of Dendur, was dedicated to the goddess Isis and to two boys, Pahor and Petesi (or Pihor and Pedesi), the sons of Quper. Quper may have been one of the leaders of the Lower Nubians who revolted at Aswan. The commemoration of his sons in this temple was one of the many ways by which Augustus paid honor to the Nubians.

Also because of the efforts of Queen Amanirenas and other Meroitic rulers, the Roman Empire and the kingdom of Meroë ceased all hostilities and enjoyed a period of peace and prosperity that was to last for the next hundred years or so. The luxury products of Africa continued to be exported by the Meroites to the far reaches of the known world.

THE FALL OF THE KINGDOM OF MEROË ▪ The kingdom of Meroë reached the peak of its success during the first century A.D. Its wealth and power came from its undisputed control of the trade routes to central Africa. That control began to be threatened during the third century, when a new group of African people established a kingdom in northern Ethiopia, with their capital at Axum.

The Axumites, as these Ethiopians are now called, realized that they were closer than the Meroites to the sources of the exotic goods of Africa. Step-by-step the Axumites gradually took over the control of the African trade routes, which had been firmly in the hands of the Nubians since the founding of the city of Kerma about 2000 B.C. The Axumites also realized that their land provided better harbors on the Red Sea for the large fleets of merchant ships plying the

The Temple of Dendur was moved to a
specially constructed wing of the Metropolitan
Museum of Art in New York City.

waters, heavily laden with the riches of India and beyond. To take advantage of this new source of income, the Axumites founded the city of Adulis, which was to become their main port. By control of the land routes and their new seaport, the Axumites gradually took over both the African and Indian trade. Meroë could no longer supply Egypt, its most important trading partner, with a continuing flow of trade goods. As a result, the economic basis on which the kingdom of Meroë had come to rely began to break down.

With a shattered economy, the Meroites could no longer keep their army in top fighting condition. As a result, bands of nomads, whose camels enabled them to master the deserts, now began to swoop down on trading caravans and villages alike. They stole things of value and threw the Meroitic economy into further confusion. By the fourth century, the Meroites could no longer defend themselves against these nomads, who seemed to gain in strength and numbers with each passing day. In time marauding hordes from the Noba tribes in the west swept into the kingdom of Meroë and occupied its towns and cities.

In the fifth century, Christian monks traveled into the region to convert the Nubians. They braved the dangers of the desert routes and attacks by nomads as they traveled southward on their missions. A century later, the Nubians had become Christian. But the history of that period and of the later rise of Islam lies outside the scope of this book, which deals with Nubia in ancient times.

EPILOGUE

THE NUBIANS TODAY

The fall of the kingdom of Meroë is but one sad chapter in the history of the Nubian people. A different, somewhat more complicated chapter began just over thirty years ago, in 1960. At that time the governments of Egypt and the Republic of Sudan decided to construct a dam across the Nile River at a point just south of the city of Aswan. One purpose of the dam was to create a large artificial lake whose waters could be used for irrigation by the farmers in both countries in times of drought. A second purpose was to harness the water so that it would fall over turbines, turning them to generate electricity. The planned lake was going to flood most of what in ancient times was Lower Nubia, one of the ancestral territories where more than 100,000 Nubians were still living at the time.

Many of these Nubians had to be resettled in Egypt on lands far removed from the banks of the Nile. In their new homes, on their new lands, the resettled Nubians still cling to their old traditions. However, today many Nubians have left their villages in search of employment opportunities and a better life. Their ancient and important cultural heritage has been preserved in part by the United Nations Educational, Scientific and Cultural Organization (UNESCO).

When Lower Nubia was about to be flooded, UNESCO appealed to the governments and the people of the world to help save

**In this village near Aswan, resettled
Nubians follow traditional ways.**

the ancient Nubian monuments. The response from many nations and many individuals was great. Teams of scientists, engineers, archaeologists, and others were sent to the area that was to be flooded. Many temples were dismantled in an effort to save them. Some, such as those at Abu Simbel, were re-erected in Nubia on higher ground, away from the rising waters of the lake. Others were shipped abroad. Among them was the Temple of Dendur, which now graces a special gallery in the Metropolitan Museum of Art in New York City.

Meanwhile, teams of archaeologists were busy excavating many of the sites and cemeteries described in this book. As a result of their work, we now know a great deal about the ancient Nubians. But there is still much that remains to be studied and analyzed. We would like to know more about the B-Group, for example. The Meroitic language remains to be deciphered.

Perhaps you, after reading this book, will decide to become an archaeologist and devote your career to the study of ancient Nubia. And maybe, just maybe, you will decipher the Meroitic language.

c. 8000–3100 B.C.	Early Nubians roam the region around the Nile River in northeastern Africa. Hunters and gatherers for thousands of years, they learn to farm about 4000 B.C.
c. 3100 B.C.	Lower Nubian villages unite to form a state. Known today as the A-Group culture, they trade with people to the north and south.
c. 2800 B.C.	Nubians and Egyptians clash over trade routes.
c. 2000–1500 B.C.	Three different Nubian cultures—the Pan-Grave, C-Group, and Kerma cultures—develop.
c. 1550 B.C.	Kerma falls to Egyptian armies. Egypt will dominate Nubia for more than five hundred years.
724 B.C.	The Nubian king Piye leads a successful invasion of Egypt. His successors rule as kings of Egypt as well as Nubia.

671 B.C.	Assyrians invade Egypt. Nubians are eventually forced to retreat to Napata, where they rule for 400 years.
c. 270 B.C.	The Nubian kingdom of Meroë is established by King Arkamani.
c. 30 B.C.–A.D. 100	The kingdom of Meroë reaches its peak of wealth and power under Candake Amanirenas and other rulers.
c. A.D. 350	Having lost control of trade routes, the kingdom of Meroë is overrun by bands of nomads.

FIND OUT MORE

To learn more about the Nubians, you may want
to visit one of the following museums, known
for their collections of Nubian art and artifacts:

The Brooklyn Museum, New York, New York

The Museum of Fine Arts, Boston, Massachusetts

The Oriental Institute Museum of the
University of Chicago, Chicago, Illinois

The Royal Ontario Museum, Toronto, Ontario, Canada

The University Museum, University of Pennsylvania,
Philadelphia, Pennsylvania

You may also want to read:

Haynes, Joyce L. *Nubia: Ancient Kingdoms of Africa.*
Boston: Museum of Fine Arts, 1992.

INDEX

Page numbers in *italics* refer to illustrations.

Abu Simbel, 57
Acculturation, 33
Adulis, 54
African rock art, 13
Afterlife, 16, 29, 34
A-Group culture, 16, 18, 24
Akinidad, Prince, 48
Amanirenas, Queen, 48–50, 52
Amenirdis, 36
Amun (god), *32*, 33, 34, 36, 40, 42, 44
Animal skulls, 19–20, *20*, 26
Apedemak (god), 44, *44*
Archaeologists, *10*, 11, 18, 57
Arkamani, King, 42, 43
Artisans, 26, 40, 46
Ashurbanipal, King, *39*, 40
Aspelta, King, 40, *41*
Assyrians, 36–38, *39*, 40
Aswan, 7, 21, 27, 34, 48, 50
Aswan Dam, 55
Augustus, Emperor, 48–50, 52
Axumites, 52, 54

Baboon deity, 16
Barter, 15

B-Group culture, 18, 57
Burials, 16, 18, 19, 38

Candakes, 48–52, *51*
Carvings, *12*, 13, 14, 21
Cattle, 14, 21, *23*, 26
C-Group culture, 19, 21–22, 27
Christianity, 54
Clothing, 16, 24, 46
Crops, 14

Dedun (god), 43
Deffufa, 24, *25*, 26

Egyptian delta, 34, 36
Egyptians, 7, 18, 22, 27–30, 33, 34, 36–38, 40, 43
Ethiopia, 11, 52

Faience, 26, 36
Farming, 11, 14–16, 46, 48
Fish, 11, 13
Floods, 8, 11
Fourth Cataract of the Nile, 22, 29
Furniture, 24

Gebel Barkal, 33
Graves, 16, 18, 19, *20*, 21, 26, 38, *39*

ABOUT THE AUTHOR

A museum professional for more than twenty years, Robert Steven Bianchi has made ancient Nubia and Egypt the focus of his work and study. In 1978, as curator of Egyptian Art at the Brooklyn Museum, he helped organize the first international loan exhibition devoted exclusively to Nubian art.

Dr. Bianchi was with the Brooklyn Museum from 1976 to 1991 and then served as J. Clawson Mills Fellow at the Egyptian Department of the Metropolitan Museum of Art in New York City. He holds master's and doctoral degrees in Greek, Roman, and Egyptian art and architecture from New York University's Institute of Fine Arts and has taught at NYU and other institutions. Dr. Bianchi has lived and studied in Egypt and travels widely to visit archaeological sites and museums with collections of ancient art. Although he has written extensively for adults, this is his first book for young readers.